Gareth Gates

Keith West

Published in association with The Basic Skills Agency

Hodder & Stoughton

A MEMBER OF THE HODDER HEADLINE GROUP

Acknowledgements
Cover: Richard Young/Rex Features

Photos: p. 3 © Richard Crampton/Rex Features; pp. 10, 14 © Brian Rasic/REX FEATURES; p. 12 © Richard Young/REX FEATURES; p. 22 © Tony Kyriacou/REX FEATURES; p. 22 © REX FEATURES.

Orders; please contact Bookpoint Ltd, 130 Milton Park, Abingdon, Oxon OX14 4SB. Telephone (44) 01235 827720, Fax: (44) 01235 400454. Lines are open from 9.00–6.00, Monday to Saturday, with a 24 hour message answering service. You can also order through our website www.hodderheadline.co.uk

British Library Cataloguing in Publication Data
A catalogue record for this title is available from the British Library

ISBN 0 340 87658 1

First published 2003
Impression number   10 9 8 7 6 5 4 3 2 1
Year   2007 2206 2005 2004 2003

Copyright © Keith West 2003

Typeset by SX Composing DTP, Rayleigh, Essex.
Printed in Great Britain for Hodder & Stoughton Educational, a division of Hodder Headline, 338 Euston Road, London NW1 3BH by The Bath Press Ltd, Bath.

Contents

1 The Musicals

Most people want to be famous.
Gareth Gates was no exception.
He wanted to be a pop star.
He wanted to make records.
Gareth had a problem.
He was born with a stammer.

As Gareth grew up
the stammer got worse.
He didn't want the stammer
to get in the way of
what he wanted to do.
He wanted to succeed.
Success does not come without hard work.
Gareth was determined to work hard.

When Gareth was 5 he took part in a musical.
The musical was called 'The King and I'.
Gareth got the part of the King's youngest son.
He had the part that made everyone laugh.

After the show people thought that
one day Gareth would become a star.

Gareth's school put on a musical.
It was called
'Joseph and the Amazing Technicolor Dreamcoat'.
Gareth was only 8.
He knew the main song from the musical.
The song was a hit record by Jason Donovan.
Gareth's teacher asked him to sing the song.
Nobody had heard Gareth sing before.
The teacher and Gareth's classmates were shocked.
He had a good voice.
He sang without a stammer.
Gareth could overcome his stammer
when he sang.

The teacher gave Gareth the main part.
He had started on the long road to fame.

Gareth has always been close to his family. Here he is singing with his sister.

2 Hard Work

Gareth wanted to play the guitar.
He worked hard in music lessons at school.
He also had private guitar lessons.
Gareth practised for an hour every day.

Gareth got involved in school concerts.
He sang solo parts in the
school concerts.

Gareth then became a choirboy.
He sang in Bradford Cathedral.
He worked hard at training his voice.
The hard work paid off after five years.

He began to practise three nights each week.
He sang every Sunday at his church.

3 Competitions

Gareth and his family had caravan holidays
every summer.
Gareth entered talent competitions.
Most young people sang pop tunes.
Gareth sang other types of songs.
He always made the finals.

When Gareth was 14 he entered
a talent show in the caravan park.
He sang 'I Will Always Love You'.
He could not hit the high notes.
His voice was breaking.

Gareth had to work on his voice.
He needed to get the lower notes.
He still wanted to be a singer.
Gareth refused to give in.

Gareth and his sister sang duets.
They entered lots of competitions.
They went on a television show
called 'Talent for Tomorrow'.

Gareth then sang for 'Steps to the Stars'.
This was yet another competition.
He made it to the final.

Gareth auditioned for a boy band.
The first round was judged on looks.
He passed!
The second round was judged on singing.
He passed!
The third round was judged on dancing.
He failed!

4 *Pop Idol*: Auditions

Gareth almost missed the
closing date for *Pop Idol*.
He filled in the form late at night.
He gave another form to his sleepy sister.

Nicola was not pleased when Gareth
woke her up and made her fill in the form.
He woke his mum up and made her drive to the
supermarket to get a passport photograph.

Nicola and Gareth needed
a passport photograph for the judges.

Gareth made Nicola sit in the booth.
He watched while the camera flashed.
Then he got a photograph for himself.
He made sure the forms were filled in.
He then posted the forms.

Gareth had a feeling *Pop Idol*
would be his breakthrough.
He started writing songs before
Pop Idol started.

The auditions were held in Manchester in
July 2001.
There were a lot of people at the auditions.
All of them wanted to be stars.
Many had not sung in front of judges before.
Some of them were very nervous.

Some of the hopeful stars were crying.
They were crying because the judges
told them they had no talent.

Gareth was not nervous.
But he had a bad stammer.
He was worried.
Pop stars don't stammer.
He need not have worried.
His singing saw him through.

5 *Pop Idol*: The Competition.

Ant and Dec presented *Pop Idol*.
It was a follow-up
series to *Pop Stars*.

There were five groups of
ten people on television
for five weeks.

Two people from each ten were
picked to go on to the next round.

The final ten had to
perform each week.
They were knocked out
until there were only two left.

Gareth with Ant and Dec.

The contestants had to perform
different kinds of songs
in different styles.
The judges gave ideas
and talked about how the
singers could improve.

The public watching at
home could vote for
their favourite singer.

The singers with the
smallest number of votes
were sent home.
The singers with the largest
amount of votes went through
to the next round.

One contestant dropped out.
His name was Rik Waller.
He was replaced by Darius Danesh.

Soon there were only
three singers left in the competition.
They were Darius Danesh, Will Young
and Gareth Gates.

The *Pop Idol* judges – Simon Cowell, Nicki Chapman and Pete Waterman.

6 *Pop Idol*: Gareth's Rivals

Darius Danesh

Darius was thought to be
cheesy but cute.
He was once a contestant
on *Pop Stars*.
He reworked the Britney Spears' song,
'Baby One More Time', and was voted out.

He did not perform well.
Even his mum was embarrassed.

Darius came third in *Pop Idol*.
Then he released a single
called 'Colour Blind'.
He wrote the song himself.
All the songs on his album, *Dive In*,
were co-written by Darius.

Darius singing at the Summer XS pop festival.

Will Young

Like Gareth, Will has auditioned for a boy band.
One day Will was watching
'This Morning' on television.
Richard and Judy wanted
to put together a new boy band.
They wanted boys who could sing.

Will applied.
The judges noticed Will's star quality.
He was picked for the band.

The band was made up of four boys.
They never became famous.
They never got a record deal.

Will knew the band was going nowhere.
He decided to pull out.

Although the band
never got famous,
it made Will realise
how much he wanted to sing.

Will saw the advert
for *Pop Idol*.
He decided to enter.

Will wore a scruffy T-shirt.
His jeans were past their best.
He did not look like a Pop Idol.
But people liked the way he sang.

Will's family travelled
to the studio to see him.
They gave him support.

He made it to the final fifty.
He went on to face Gareth in the final.
Now Will and Gareth sing together.

Will has released an album.

Will and Gareth both have a great future
thanks to *Pop Idol*.

Will and Gareth at the *Pop Idol* final.

7 *Pop Idol*: Gareth Gates

Gareth sang a Westlife song.
It was called 'Flying Without Wings'.
The judges liked his singing.
He made it to the final fifty.

He sang in front of millions
of viewers for weeks.
He made it to the final.

But he lost to Will Young.

Gareth sang 'Unchained Melody'.
He sang the song well.
Many people thought he
would win *Pop Idol*.

Four million people voted
for Gareth but over four million
voted for Will.

Gareth promised his supporters that
he would work hard to become a star.

He would not give up just
because he came second.

Gareth's mum is called Wendy.
She thought the judges
were shocked when he came second.

Some people could not vote.
The telephone lines were blocked for 2 hours.
Wendy had to fight back tears.
She had always thought Gareth would win.

Gareth was disappointed.
He really wanted to win *Pop Idol*.
He thought he sang the
songs as well as he could.
He performed his best.

It was not to be.

Pop Idol gave Gareth confidence.
It gave him the confidence
to go on and become a star.

He had gained experience.
He was able to sing every week on television.
Gareth had learned to cope with his stammer.
He had to be a strong person to cope.
He had proved he could cope.

Gareth had worked on his music all his life.
He had worked on his voice.
He had learned how to write songs.
Gareth had worked on playing a guitar.

Now the dream had come true.
Nobody lost out.

The record company
signed a deal with
Will Young and Gareth Gates.

Both stars had fulfilled their dreams.
Both stars would earn a lot of money.
Both stars would be famous.

8 Fame

Everybody wants to know all
they can about Gareth Gates.
He is now famous.
His moment has come.

He has many fans.
Letters arrive in the post every day.

He has been to Florida
with his record company.

Fame has not stopped Gareth
caring for others.
He still wants to help other people.
He is still a Christian.

Gareth singing at the *Pop Idol* concert, Wembley Arena.

9 Being A Star

Being a star is not all glamour.
There are good and bad times.
Gareth has met both already.

The upside of being a star:

In 2002, Gareth travelled to Bradford.
He returned to his home town.
He switched on the Christmas lights.

More than 20,000 fans
were there to see Gareth.
They wanted to cheer
as he turned on the lights.

He sang his No. 1 hit
'Suspicious Minds'.
The crowd cheered.

The <u>downside</u> of being a star:

Some people claim Gareth
is not keeping to his choir-boy image.

People also claim Gareth has a mystery lover.
Jordan claims Gareth
has spent time with her.

A newspaper claimed Gareth was
in love with Mandy Davies.
Mandy is a niece of Geri Halliwell.
Geri is a former Spice Girl.
Mandy is a member of a pop group
called Frenzy.

There are lots of rumours about Gareth.
Perhaps some of the rumours are true.
Perhaps they are not.

Fame will always bring a downside.

Gareth will need to
handle bad press.
He will not be able to stop nasty rumours.
It is all part of being famous.

Some music writers say
Gareth is a flash in the pan.
That he will fade.

There are boys who are jealous of Gareth.
They envy his success.

Many boys try to look like Gareth.
They dye their hair his colour.
They dress like him.

It is all part of being a pop star.
It is all part of being famous.

10 The Future

'Unchained Melody' was at
No. 1 for four weeks.
It sold over 1.5 million copies.
It was a cover of the
Righteous Brothers' song.

When the single was released,
Gareth was nervous.
He was in Birmingham.
He sat in a small room.
The radio was in his hand.
He heard the chart countdown.
He heard the presenter say:
'At No. 1, it's Gareth Gates!'

Gareth had fulfilled a dream.

Gareth followed that up with
another hit single.

The single was called 'Anyone Of Us'.
It is about a lover.
The lover wants his girlfriend
to forgive him.
The song is very romantic.

Gareth soon followed that up with
'A Long And Winding Road.'
This was once sung by The Beatles.
The song 'Suspicious Minds'
was also released.
This was once sung by Elvis Presley.

Gareth is often compared to Elvis.
He was pleased to sing an Elvis song.

He has also sung with Will Young.
Their duet made it to No. 1.

His debut album was released on
28 October 2002.
The album was called
What My Heart Wants To Say.

Gareth has done well.
He is certainly a pop idol now.

He will produce more albums.
Perhaps he will be as famous as
Elvis Presley.

What about you?
Have you any
ambitions to be a star?
If you want to be a star
you will need to work hard.

You will need to work
as hard as Gareth Gates.